SCHIRMER'S LIBRARY
OF MUSICAL CLASSICS

Vol. 1993

ROBERT SCHUMANN

Album For The Young

Op. 68

For Piano

Edited by
HAROLD BAUER

ISBN 978-0-7935-2994-0

G. SCHIRMER, Inc.

DISTRIBUTED BY

HAL•LEONARD
CORPORATION

7777 W. BLUEMOUND RD. P.O. BOX 13819 MILWAUKEE, WI 53213

CONTENTS

If we accept the theory of Saint-Beuve that one cannot judge the work of a man without a knowledge of the man himself, the student of Schumann should first of all become saturated with the musical ideas of Schumann, as expressed in his literary articles, and with the knowledge of the influences that controlled him. When Schumann began his career, it was an age of superficial pianoforte music and "honey-daubing" criticism. Against these evils he fought in his music journal and in his compositions.

He was pre-eminently a thinker for the pianoforte. At first this instrument was the chief vehicle of his thought. Then came the song period of his life, but in his songs the pianoforte is very important, often dominating. When he wrote for the orchestra, the thought was that of the pianist: the ideas that sprang from his brain were not clothed at the time in orchestral dress.

His pianoforte compositions show the influence of Jean Paul, E. T. A. Hoffmann, Paganini. His technique was mainly the result of private study of Bach. At the beginning he did not value form as it is commonly understood. In his earlier compositions free rein is given to fantasy. Musical pictures are painted with Flemish detail. We find glowing passion, depth of feeling, mysticism, the grotesque, sanity and insanity contained within a little space; or, as Saint-Saëns has finely said, Schumann knew how to be great within narrow limits. "Where Mendelssohn painted water-colors, Schumann cut cameos."

The style of Schumann, with its singular polyphony, with its development of pianoforte-color, is his own. It was unknown before his day. By it he founded a new romantic school. This new polyphony is shown rather in the works of small dimensions than in the Sonatas which, although they are filled with beauties, are lacking as a whole in unity. The Pianoforte Concerto, one of his greatest works, is an exception; it stands on a level with the Pianoforte Quintet and the noble and lawless Fantasia, Op. 17. The true disciple of Schumann will find keener pleasure in the compositions where the musician appears as the fiery Florestan, the dreamy Eusebius, or the sorrow-laden Johannes Kreisler. The "Papillons", the "Carnaval", the "Davidsbündler", the "Kreisleriana", the pieces for children, fantastic, romantic, humorous (to use the Elizabethan phrase)—these are revelations to the world of Schumann as he was influenced by himself, his surroundings, his friendships with authors and women. The music says with Whitman, "I am the man, I suffered, I was there."

It has been claimed, and justly, that Schumann demands a special technique for interpretation. It is also true that he demands a player of peculiar temperament. There must be a thoroughly developed mechanism as well as a keen appreciation of rhythmic difficulties. This mechanism must be the servant of a poet of "fine frenzy". Gagnière in Zola's "L'Oeuvre" apostrophized Schumann as "despair, the joy of despair! Yes, the end of all things, the last song of mournful purity, soaring over the ruins of the world!" But this despair is only one of the elements of a music that challenges even the supreme pianist-poet.

PHILIP HALE

The foregoing biographical sketch, written by the well-known critic Philip Hale, and reprinted from the 1893 Schirmer edition, will help the reader to understand the importance of that period in Schumann's life during which the "Album for the Young" was composed. This set of pieces, originally called "Christmas Album", dates from 1848, when Schumann had already written all of his greatest piano works, a large number of songs, most of his chamber music, and many other compositions. He was consequently at his fullest maturity.

On more than one occasion, he had expressed the thought that posterity might attach more value to the pieces he wrote for little children than to his larger works. Of Op. 68 he said that it had given him "indescribable joy" to compose these miniatures. "I felt as if I were beginning composition all over again," we find in a letter to Carl Reinecke. He also remarked that these pieces differ radically from the "Kinderscenen", which are "reminiscences of an older person", whereas the "Album for the Young" is to be regarded as "anticipations and experiences of young people".

The first numbers of this collection were composed especially for the birthday of Robert's and Clara's eldest child, and the other pieces were added later. From 1 to 18 they are intended solely for young folk, and it is understood that from 19 to 43 the youngsters are on the way to becoming "grown-ups".

None of these delightful miniatures call for extended comment. The pieces without title, each one headed by a group of three stars, offer some food for speculation and seem to indicate (in the present writer's opinion) that Schumann was offering more than a single tribute to the memory of his beloved friend Mendelssohn, whose style is perfectly imitated not only in "Erinnerung" (In Memoriam) but in these three other pieces as well. On November 4, 1848, Robert wrote to his friend, Johannes Verhulst: "Everybody is here again—except the One who was the best of all. It is exactly a year ago today since he departed from us." This refers to the death of Felix Mendelssohn, and it seems quite probable that "Erinnerung" was written on the same date as the letter.

H. B.

PREFACE

Robert Alexander Schumann was born at Zwickau, in Saxony, June 8, 1810. His father was a book-seller, who encouraged the musical inclination of his son. His mother was an affectionate woman, sensible in worldly affairs, who, although she looked askew at the life of an artist, was romantic to the verge of sentimentalism. The boy, according to his own account, began to compose music before he was seven years old. It is probable that he studied the pianoforte at an earlier date. His first teacher was Kuntzsch, a church organist at Zwickau, who prophesied the greatness of his pupil whose improvisation was even then regarded as remarkable. During the winter of 1817-18 his father asked Carl Maria von Weber to look after his son. Weber was willing, but the scheme was abandoned. The father died in 1826.

Loyal to his mother's wish, Schumann studied in the gymnasium, and in 1828 he matriculated at the University of Leipzig as *Studiosus Juris*. In Leipzig he first met and studied under Friedrich Wieck, the pianoforte teacher. There was a struggle between law, which he loathed, and music, which he loved. But he was even then disinclined to theoretical study in music; for music was to him a language for the outward expression of mental ideas, and form seemed the choker of spontaneity. In 1829 he went to Heidelberg University, where he was industrious chiefly in pianoforte playing. He practised seven hours a day. When he drove, he took a dumb pianoforte with him in the carriage. His only appearance in public was at a concert in Heidelberg, where he played the variations on the "Alexandermarsch", by Moscheles. In 1830 he went back to Leipzig; he studied the pianoforte under Wieck and composition under Dorn. He gave promise of becoming a virtuoso of the first rank, but after a year's study, one of the fingers of his right hand was crippled by the use of a contrivance of his for equalizing the strength of the fingers. In 1840 the University of Jena gave him the degree of Ph.D.; and in the same year he married Clara Wieck. The courtship had been long and anxious, and it is not unlikely that Wieck's opposition was inspired by knowledge of Schumann's diseased brain, for the disease had declared itself when he was twenty-three years old.

In 1834 he was largely instrumental in founding the *Neue Zeitschrift für Musik*, and he was sole editor of it from 1835 to 1844.

The Leipzig conservatory was founded in 1843, and Schumann was for a time instructor in score-reading. In 1844 he moved to Dresden, where in 1847 he conducted the Liedertafel and in 1848 founded the Chorgesangverein. In 1850 he was appointed city music-director of Düsseldorf. His disease grew upon him. In 1853 he resigned his position. Insanity broke out on February 6, 1854, when Schumann threw himself into the Rhine. He was rescued and taken to a private asylum at Endenich, near Bonn. There were a few lucid intervals during the last two years of his life. He died July 29, 1856.

Album for the Young
43 Piano Pieces

Edited by
Harold Bauer

Robert Schumann, Op. 68
Composed in 1848

1. Melody

8

2. Soldiers' March

3. Humming Song

4. Choral

5. Little Piece

6. The Poor Orphan

7. Hunting Song

8. The Wild Horseman

9. Folk Song

10. The Happy Farmer

returning from work

11. Sicilienne

Fine

D.C. senza repetizione al Fine

12. Knecht Ruprecht*

13. May, Sweet May

14. Little Study

*Originally in $\frac{6}{8}$ time. The editor has altered the notation to **C** (i.e. two measures in one) in order to indicate with greater clarity the rhythmical pulse of the piece.

15. Spring Song

16. First Loss

17. Roaming in the Morning

18. The Reaper's Song

19. Little Romance

20. Rustic Song

21. Lento Espressivo

*In the original this piece is headed by three stars: ✳ ✳ ✳

22. Roundelay

Moderato ♩. = 76

23. The Horseman

24. Harvest Song

25. Echoes from the Theatre

Poco agitato ♩= 96

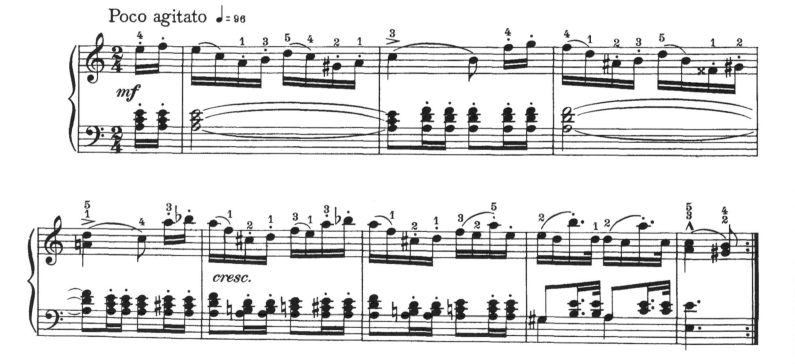

26. Andante Con Moto

*In the original this piece is headed by three stars: ✳ ✳ ✳

27. Little Song in Canon-form

Andante molto espressivo ♩= 60

28. In Memoriam

November 4th, 1847*

29. Strange Man

Vigoroso con forza ♩=126

30. Molto Lento

31. War Song

32. Sheherazade

33. Vintage-time

34. Theme

35. Mignon

36. Italian Sailors' Song

37. Sailors' Song

* Execution:

38. Winter-time (I)

39. Winter-time (II)

Poco a poco più animato

(a) and (b) The keen listener will not fail to observe these two sly allusions to the Seventeenth-Century "Grossvater Tanz" used by Schumann in both "Papillons" and "Carnaval".

40. Little Fugue

Prelude

Allegro moderato ♩=96

Fugue

Animato, ma non troppo ♩. = 80

41. Norse Song

Greeting to G*

In the style of a folk-song ♩= 72

*Niels W. Gade (Danish composer and friend of Schumann)

42. Figured Choral

*It will be noticed that the theme is identical with that of the simple "Choral", No. 4 in this album.

43. New Year's Eve